MW00953808

Press On

Encouragement to Keep You Moving When You Feel Overwhelmed

Gretchen Fleming

Following Hard Press
Jacksonville, Florida

Gretchen Fleming/Following Hard Press

www.gretchenfleming.com

Press On: Encouragement to Keep You Moving When You Feel Overwhelmed

ISBN-13: 978-1977765581

Scriptures taken from the Holy Bible, New International Version®, NIV®. Copyright © 1973, 1978, 1984, 2011 by Biblica, Inc.™ Used by permission of Zondervan. All rights reserved worldwide. **www.zondervan.com** The "NIV" and "New International Version" are trademarks registered in the United States Patent and Trademark Office by Biblica, Inc.™

Table of Contents

Introduction

Do you know what has the power to strengthen your perseverance? Perspective! It is fuel for perseverance, greatly influencing our stamina.

So, if you are weary or overwhelmed, then join me for 14 days of devotions. You will find a new perspective that can make all the difference! I have found that God can do great things IN us even as we wait for Him to do great things FOR us. Seeking His wisdom and perspective opens us up to more than just the rescue desperately needed.

Truly, our entire perspective of what concerns us can be changed in an instant. Our greatest need can actually become secondary. What we may see as a problem, God sees as His purpose for bringing about our freedom as He transforms us into Christlikeness. He patiently enables us to respond differently to what we find so unbearable.

What used to hinder our perseverance can be cast aside as we learn from Christ how to process our pain. Through Him, we can find our means of strength and joy for the journey.

Along with reading each of the devotions from the Old Testament, you can make this experience more effective by trying these things:

- Look up the mentioned scriptures in your Bible. Read and meditate on each of the passages.
- Spend time praying over all that you read.
- Ask questions each day - What does God want me to do with what I have read? How can I apply this lesson?
- Add a gratitude journal into your daily routine. Begin your devotions with making a list of what you have to be thankful for from the previous day. Focus on what IS praiseworthy today.
- Share one thing you learn each day with a friend or family member. This will cement some of these truths into your heart.

I'm praying that God will greatly encourage you through your experiences with this book, giving you strength for what is required of you today. Thank you for joining me here!

Gretchen

About The Author

About Me

As a wife (29 years) and mother (25 years), life has taught me many lessons. Through personal and family challenges, I have experienced breaking points and had to fight hard to stand firm in my faith through God's sustaining grace.

My Passion

My passion is to follow hard after Jesus, knowing He is the treasure of a lifetime and worth every minute I commit to Him. God's Word has been life giving through the most trying times—a great source of strength, wisdom, and truth. It is my heartfelt desire to encourage women in their faith with the hope I have found in His Word.

My Ministry

I am a Bible study teacher, writer, and speaker who loves to see Jesus change lives as He's changed mine.

It's a joy to share with others the Truth that can give us perspective and perseverance, no matter what we face.

My Website

You can find more words of encouragement on my website. Head over to **www.gretchenfleming.com**

Day 1

Eyes to See the Hope Before Us

(Joshua 6:1-2; Joshua 9:14-15)

One of the most life-changing truths I have learned from studying God's Word these last 25 years has been about perspective and how it can bring about my victory or my defeat, my hope or my despair, my perseverance or my failure.

It has literally been the difference, emotionally and spiritually, between life and death for me.

The understanding of perspective that has made such a difference in my life comprises two key principles and Joshua gives great examples of both.

Joshua 6:1-2 says,

Now Jericho was securely shut up because of the children of Israel; none went out, and none came in.

And the LORD said to Joshua: "See! I have given Jericho into your hand, its king, and the mighty men of valor.

"Wow! Really? That's not what it looks like to me. It looks 'tightly shut up' and not exactly 'delivered' from where I am standing."

That is what would have been going through my mind if I were Joshua at that moment.

But this offers a perfect example of the first principle to learn: **the difference in perspective.** This difference boils down to God's view versus our view.

I have seen over and over in Scripture how differently He sees and processes compared to humans. This has had a profound impact to teach me that more often than not, as I approach any given situation, my initial view may be flawed, biased or incomplete. I have learned to recognize my vulnerability when it comes to perceiving and processing life.

This shouldn't surprise me though. God affirms it in His Word.

Proverbs 3:5 teaches,

> *Trust in the LORD with all your heart*
> *and lean not on your own understanding;*

Later in Isaiah 55:9, I learn,

As the heavens are higher than the earth,
so are my ways higher than your ways and my thoughts
than your thoughts.

These two verses illustrate how God perceives and processes not just differently, but oh so much better than I ever can! Therefore, when I am looking at whatever situation is in front of me, I know there is more than one way to see everything.

As in the case with Joshua looking at Jericho, what he saw "tightly shut up", God saw as already delivered!!

Let that sink in, savoring all the hope it offers!

What we see as overwhelming or impossible, God sees as already accomplished! What we see as pointless or painful, God sees as purposeful!

Why? Because He is God! Almighty and Invincible! All-Loving and All-wise! Nothing can stump Him and nothing can stop Him!

He can and will use absolutely everything for our ultimate good (Romans 8:28). No exceptions!

What comfort that offers us when we struggle. But it doesn't just stop there. Not only are we blessed by God having a better perspective of any given situation than what we are able to, when we seek that perspective and align ourselves with it, our circumstance is as good as changed. One way or another!

Therefore, the second principle to learn is **the value His in perspective**.

Whether it is a different way to perceive a circumstance left unchanging for the time God allows, or by seeking instruction on how to deal with it more strategically, there is value in pursuing God's perspective.

That is exactly what Joshua and the Israelites learned the hard way in Joshua 9:14-15. The people of Gibeon came to the Israelites in a ruse, seeking a treaty with them, knowing they were probably next on their list to annihilate. They pretended to live far away and asked for protection through a treaty and oath.

Upon hearing this, it says in verse 14-15,

> *The Israelites sampled their provisions but did not inquire of the LORD. Then Joshua made a treaty of peace with them to let them live, and the leaders of the assembly ratified it by oath.*

It was only a matter of time before Joshua learned that the Gibeonites were actually a neighboring nation that should have been conquered. The Israelites were to take possession of their land as God had intended and rid the potential influence of its inhabitants.

They had failed to seek God's perspective on the matter, making the decision themselves in their flawed, vulnerable reasoning. The LORD wanted to equip them but they had not valued His perspective enough to ask. Therefore, they missed out on the better way God had intended for them.

I have suffered the same losses in my life, more times than I care to count. Having neglected to seek His view on circumstances so that I could enjoy what my own flesh wanted instead, I foolishly thought I could handle "this one" on my own. Now at 51, I am more prone to seek His view or instruction.

When I am in the midst of this difficult state of waiting, vulnerable to feeling hopeless or fearful, I try to remember the difference in perspective from more than two thousand years ago; the difference between the second and third day for the disciples after Jesus was crucified.

On the second day, they must have been reeling with confusion, fear, and despair. Helpless and hopeless would have described them well as they hid themselves from the Jews, trying to process what had just happened, what the last three years had been about. You see, their perspective from in front of the cross on that day of crucifixion or from inside their homes as they hid the next day, was incomplete.

Oh, how their view was about to change that next morning. Their perspective would radically shift just hours later!

The view from His empty tomb made all the difference! What had happened at Calvary had been totally changed in their minds by the fact that now He had risen. He wasn't defeated; He was victorious!!

That meant so were they!!

And so are we my friends!

The difference in perspective makes all things hopeful for us. We are not left mourning as the disciples were on the second day.

We are more than conquerors because He has conquered sin and death on our behalf! What more can stand in our way? If He is not stumped, we are not stumped. If He is not stopped, we are not stopped.

So be encouraged as you seek Him. Wait for His perspective and remember the view from inside the tomb!!

Day 2

Digging Deep to Not Give Up

(Numbers 21)

We are all waiting for something.

We're holding on for a hope, a dream, a resolution, or an answer to prayer that's very dear to us.

No one gets a pass. It doesn't matter how blessed we may be, there is something "more" we desperately desire. Whether it is regarding a relationship, a healing, a ministry, a provision of income or opportunity, we can fixate on that one thing needed.

If you have been waiting a long time, you know the weariness or discouragement that can set in. You know the temptation to give up in despair.

Impatience is like the pressure mounting in a teakettle on the verge of boiling.

At varying times in our "wait", impatience seems to come to a boiling point where we feel we are going to explode if we have to wait ONE MORE DAY!

We can begin to grumble and complain wondering if what we are waiting for will EVER become a reality. Impatience has a way of providing an open door to all kinds of negative emotions. It allows these emotions to enter our hearts and minds as we stew over not having what we want.

Bitterness and cynicism can become our unwelcome friends if we are not diligent.

For the Israelites in Numbers 21, their "wait" involved traveling with recurring needs that their environment could not supply. The scarcity of food and water in the desert forced them to look to God for provision of daily necessities, what they could not do for themselves.

And isn't that the rub?

Waiting for what we are powerless to do for ourselves-nobody likes that feeling of helplessness. It says in Numbers 21:4 that the people travelled along the route to the Red Sea (yes, back to where they had already been).

It should be remembered that they could be in their promised land by now had they not rebelled (in fear of the inhabitants of the land) by refusing to go in. I am sure their own frustrations with themselves weighed in on them, coupled with going back toward their original starting point.

Therefore, it should come as no surprise that "the people grew impatient on the way".

Boy, doesn't that describe us?

We are impatient on our way, the journey that God has us on. I know! Believe me, I know how the enemy tempts us to doubt if our lives will ever reflect the change we hope to come.

We begin to think we are fools if we continue to hope, dream, or pray. We ponder giving up- the only probable answer for the relief of the pressure mounting within us from impatience.

But I want to tell you dear brothers and sisters in Christ to dig deep!! Do not give up!!

God is ALWAYS worth the wait!

The plans He has for us are the best for us, worth waiting for and submitting to, for His Glory and our ultimate gain. We may or may not gain what we think is our particular future in mind, but we can rest assured His will IS for our ultimate good.

The Israelites wallowed in their negative emotions, sinning against God because of it. We must learn from their mistakes and turn that desperation or impatience into what propels us to the throne of God.

We must go to Him with all the unrest in our hearts and minds, laying them at His feet. Psalm 55:22 says,

> *Cast your cares on the LORD*
> *and he will sustain you;*
> *he will never let*
> *the righteous be shaken.*

We don't have to dig deep and feel better on our own. We must dig deep to run to Him, time and again, until we have the desire of our heart OR He changes the desire we have.

When we fail to keep turning to God, casting our cares on Him for help, we will give way to impatience just as the Israelites did.

How do I go to Him for this?

I go by praying, turning to His Word for strength, comfort and perspective, listening to uplifting worship music, and by looking through my gratitude journal to remember all He has done for me at other times. Sometimes, I call my prayer partners whom I know will lift me up in my time of weakness.

We don't have to see the exact way God will answer our desire in order to continue to have faith. All we need to do is remember He is I AM. Therefore, He is able to do what we cannot even conceive AND in an instant.

Our hope becoming our reality could happen tomorrow, dear ones, so dig deep and do not give up! Let impatience thrust you back to His throne for the strength you need to wait one more day!

Day 3

Crying Out to God

(1 Samuel 1)

"In bitterness of soul Hannah wept much and prayed to the Lord."

What emotions are evoked from those words! In reading them, I can feel the depth of her heartache, the desperation of her soul.

Oh, if only she could change her situation!

Hannah was a barren woman desperate for a child of her own in 1 Samuel 1:1-10. Year after year, when they would go for the annual sacrifice to worship, it would also remind her that it had been one more year without a child.

Each time they went, it drove her grief deeper, her desperation greater.

Her rival made it even worse. Her husband had another wife who had plenty of children.

Knowing that the husband favored Hannah, she made it her goal to provoke Hannah, inflicting much torment, as only a woman can when feeling the sting of jealousy over a man's affections.

Hannah would get into such an emotional state that she would be unable to eat at the feast. Her anguish from her barrenness and her rival's gloating overshadowed all else. It consumed her.

She was broken, helpless to remedy her heart's desire of her own accord.

Have you been there? Can you relate to her angst as she longs for a particular desire? I know I can. I know that moment with the Lord. I remember it clearly.

That grief, that depth of helplessness and frustration, isn't where I want to return anytime soon. I had not just one situation driving me to my undoing but two. And I was equally incapable of changing either circumstance.

I remember crying many tears and praying often because what else could I do?

What else could Hannah do?

When you are helpless, well..... you are helpless. And time is not your friend. Waiting can be excruciating.

Time spent crying before the Lord is not passive though, nor is it wasted. Though painful, it is still productive, even purifying. It can be a time of testimony as Hannah demonstrated in verses 9-15.

We learn that this time before the Lord is demonstrative of two other spiritual implications. It says in verse 9 that Hannah "stood up" while they were at the feast in Shiloh, giving the impression that everyone else remained seated. It was as if she could not sit for one more minute while others were enjoying the celebration yet she was so miserable.

She had to flee that physical place by running to her Lord inwardly, to a spiritual place. She stood up and began to weep and pray. Hannah was taking her stand in the only way she could- IN HOPE.

Psalm 130:7 describes what Hannah was doing.

> *Israel, put your hope in the LORD,*
> *for with the LORD is unfailing love*
> *and with him is full redemption.*

She knew that with the Lord, there is always hope. Because of His great love for His people, for her, hope remains possible even in an impossible situation. God had the power to demonstrate the depth of His love. He was the one who could alter her situation so she steadfastly took her stand with that knowledge.

She defied her situation by standing firm in what she knew.

This reminds me of one of the songs that ministered to me the most when I was in my season of crying before the Lord. I would listen and feel more determined than ever, God was not going to fail me. One way or another, this side of heaven or the other, God was going to make all things right. As I cried before the Lord, I was just as much digging my heels in with hope.

Additionally, crying before the Lord also represents our dependence on Him as we wait in hope. He is the only One to sustain us in our desperation. When all we want to do is give up and stay in bed with the covers pulled over our heads, while life demands our continued commitment and involvement, we turn to Him and find the strength needed to persevere.

Hannah didn't just cry, she turned to the Lord in prayer and in faith. Her grief was given to the One who could help bear her burden.

In my most difficult days, I would walk my neighborhood and play certain songs over and over. I knew I was hanging on by a thread at times yet I recognized Who could keep the grip even when I could not. Those songs represented what I was doing; turning to the Lord, crying out for mercy.

When we are crying before the Lord, it is not a hopeless act void of purpose. Hannah understood the testimony of faith and commitment it represented. She was His child, and He was her God. With the Lord, not one tear goes unnoticed.

When we turn to Him in bitterness of soul, He can take it. There is an intimacy that is forged in those desperate moments that bears fruit for a lifetime afterward.

Therefore, with hope and dependence, let us stand firm in what we know, reaping the benefits of His unfailing love, even as we continue to wait.

Day 4

Finding Strength in the Lord

(1 Samuel 30)

Do you ever feel overwhelmed? In over your head? Swamped by what you face?

David knew that feeling well. In 1 Samuel 30, he had been on the run from his enemies for far too long. He had been wrongly accused and pursued, facing danger from men and armies alike as he tried to stay one step ahead of those who were determined to end his life.

At this particular time, David and his men were returning to Ziklag, their home base while they were hiding from King Saul in the Philistine area. They were already vulnerable as they sought to be double agents in enemy territory. They pretended to be friends with the Philistines, all the while raiding their towns, leaving no one to testify against them to the leaders of that nation.

In reality, they lived in danger of the nation Israel, under King Saul's command, as well as the Philistines. They were caught between a rock and a hard place.

As they lived under that stress, it was no wonder that they took it hard when they returned home only to find out that the Amalekites had raided them. As they entered the town, seeing it burned and destroyed, they were devastated. All of their wives and children were gone. They had been taken captive.

It says in verse 4 that David and his men wept aloud until they had no strength left to weep. Can you imagine battle weary men bawling their eyes out? Do you know that staggering feeling of an unexpected blow, when you are already depleted and hanging on by a thread? I do.

There have been times in recent years when all I could do was try and keep my head above water. At those times I was most vulnerable, a rogue wave would hit me from out of nowhere. Feeling on the verge of going under from the strain of life's circumstances, it was almost impossible not to give way and feel absolutely abandoned, overwhelmed.

That feeling left me gasping for air at times, as if someone had just punched me in the gut.

I can relate with how David and his men wept until they had no strength left.

To make matters worse, it says that David was greatly distressed because his men were talking of stoning him, as each one was "bitter in spirit because of his sons and daughters". They had given way to despair and what is all too predictable- blaming whomever they could at the moment. They were turning on him, seeking to satisfy their anger and vengeance.

But what happens next in verse 6 is remarkable!

When all of this was crashing down upon David, losing his own family and having all his men speak of stoning him, he responded contrary to his circumstances. It says, "But David found strength in the LORD his God".

Wow!

How does that happen? How can someone in such overwhelming circumstances find strength?

I notice immediately the word "but" as it described David's response. That word lets me know how unusual David was. He did what no one else did. He "found strength in the LORD".

How did he actually do that?

I immediately go back to some of his most recent Psalms that he wrote during that particular time.

They give needed context and instruction. His Psalms give an up-close and personal view of what was going on in his heart and mind, giving insight into how he persevered so well.

I notice a pattern in most of them. He usually testifies of who God is, what he knows to be truth about the Lord. He recites His character and ability, then he calls upon His help. He laments what he is facing while he ascribes the attributes of God that can help him. He acknowledges his difficulties or crises, but *he keeps moving forward with how God is more than able to handle it all.*

His pattern is that he *describes the desperate nature of his circumstances but counters with the All-Sufficient nature of his God.*

Psalm 69:29-30 is a good example of this. David exclaims that he is in distress and pleads God's salvation to protect him.

Then the very next verse he says,

I will praise God's name in song
and glorify him with thanksgiving.

This teaches me how he found strength in the Lord.

First, he turned to the Lord. He did not lament purposelessly. He turned to the One who loved him and who could make a difference.

Secondly, he reminded himself of who God was, His character and abilities. This in turn always portrayed his God to be greater than whatever he faced. It set his perspective correctly, because left to our own vision of the reality in front of us we begin to think the issues are insurmountable.

But by remembering our God, we gain valuable perspective that actually produces hope and encouragement in us.

Thirdly, he always praised and worshipped the Lord and this was done progressively. *He praised more than he fretted!* It does not escape my notice that *he chose* to praise.

It was not always easy, but as in verse 30, David said, "I will praise....".

I am so captivated by the One who not only gives us examples of others in the Word, but also uses it to teach us how to benefit from their life story. David was one of the greatest when it came to perseverance and devotion. He endured, overcoming his breaking point and now we know how- because he found strength in the Lord his God!

What about you? Are you near your breaking point? Are you feeling utterly inadequate for what you face?

Remember the lessons of David and you can be the exception to the norm as he was. While others may give way and fold under the pressure, you can find strength in the Lord and overcome!

Day 5

How Our Immediate Response to a Crisis Can Be Our Best

(1 Samuel 21-23)

What is our knee-jerk response to what frightens us?

When my children were in preschool, we lived out in the country amongst farmland. It was quite and safe so they were allowed the freedom to roam or play as I worked in the yard. Because our home was set back from the road, half the time I would be outside still in my nightgown as I went about my chores for the day.

Country life had its perks!

One day, the three children were scattered around the property playing- one with a shovel, one with a hose and one on a bike, when all of a sudden a roaring sound developed. It was impossible to ascertain which direction the sound was coming from but it was getting louder and louder.

Nothing could be seen only the roar could be heard.

As an adult, I knew what the sound was because I had heard it before in other places, but my children had no idea.

As I lifted my head hearing the beginning of the sound, I saw all three of my children INSTANTLY drop what they were doing and run as fast as they could to grab hold of my gown.

Not one of them made a sound! They just instinctively ran for their mama in the confusion of the moment.

It was like watching a National Geographic show where baby animals behave instinctively! Their knee-jerk reaction was to run for cover.

It is noteworthy that they did not run to the porch or inside the house for protection.

They ran to me.

WHY?

They knew my instinct was to protect them fiercely!

They didn't understand military jets or their powerful engines at the time because they didn't need to!

All they needed to know was that they had a mama who would watch over them.

What sent David into chaos and confusion?

As I am reading about David in 1 Samuel 21-23 and the corresponding Psalms (35,57,7), I see the same scenario at play.

He is confused, even panic-stricken, over the turn of events since his anointing by Samuel. David had been chosen (by God) as the next King of Israel; however, there would be a wait for him until he ascended the throne.

Meanwhile, as faithful as he had been to King Saul and the nation, he was being hunted down for execution because of jealousy.

Betrayed, pursued, and rejected, this was not what he envisioned as the chosen king. He was in fear of his life as strangers and "friends" alike sought his death.

How did David respond to these overwhelming circumstances?

He ran for cover, just like my children had.

He ran for the refuge of his Heavenly Father as described in Psalm 57:1,

I will take refuge in the shadow of your wings until the disaster has passed.

Many of the Psalms David wrote during his life are filled with descriptions of his turning to the Lord for strength and help.

I happily admit that David is my most favorite Old Testament character because of his passion and devotion to the Lord. His life is flawed at times, but he continuously turns to seek the Lord.

Additionally, he worships the Lord in his Psalms just as hard as he cries out to Him for help.

Why did he respond this way?

What was the reason David kept running to the Lord? Why did he wholeheartedly pursue God, in good times and bad?

Because of the intimacy!

As he had spent a lifetime (beginning in his teenage years) building his relationship with God, he began to receive the payoff. *What started because of duty, reading the Scriptures and praying, in time developed into a passion.*

A transaction had begun taking place.

It changed from David solely "giving" through obedience to "receiving " love and joy, among many other attributes experienced.

What was one of the main contributing factors for this taking place?

Time!

David would never have experienced all the intimacy with the Lord without all the time he had put in.

He knew instinctively what to do when life abruptly changed into what was unrecognizable. He ran for cover because He knew his God so well.

With time comes depth, and with depth comes confidence.

Just as my young children had confidence because of the time they had spent with me- they were confused and fearful of what was happening, but they were sure of me.

What about you? When unexpected events such as death or loss, betrayal or injustice, reach your sphere of life, where do you turn?

We may feel protected or immune to some storms as we strive to live in our safe little bubbles, but tragedy can come find us anywhere. Then what?

I want to stress that intimacy with God is rarely gained through reading just a short devotional in hand or with a quick app. The tendency of our day to flit here and there with our time and attention is not conducive to hard-earned intimacy.

Reading more words written ABOUT Scripture than the Scripture itself is risky.

If that is the only way we spend time with the Lord, I will venture to say that our strength, confidence, and intimacy with God will be little compared to the level that David experienced.

There is a pay off when we run for cover to the One who is Sovereign and His love unfailing. But that transaction is received to the depth that it has been prepared.

Spending regular time in the Word itself primes the pump to flow readily for those times of unexpected, life-altering events. As we read about God in the Bible, we learn about Him more and more. With time comes knowledge, and with knowledge comes intimacy.

To know Him is to love Him!

<u>Is this what you want?</u>

When life hits hard and changes our future in a heartbeat that is when we reap the level of intimacy we have sought to build. We reap what we have sown in our attentiveness to the Lord.

And what a payoff it is- to know instinctively where to run when the mountains shake and our world gives way! Psalm 142:5-7 describes it like this.

> *I cry to you, LORD;*
> *I say, "You are my refuge,*
> *my portion in the land of the living."*

Listen to my cry,
for I am in desperate need;
rescue me from those who pursue me,
for they are too strong for me.
Set me free from my prison,
that I may praise your name.
Then the righteous will gather about me
because of your goodness to me.

Day 6

2 Ways for Successfully Waiting Upon God

(2 Samuel 5)

<u>Why do we want to control time</u>?

Successfully waiting can seem impossible, not to mention excruciating!

Oh, how we long to control the hands of time! At least I do anyway. Rarely does it feel like "timing" is just right. Some seasons of life take way too long while others go much too fast.

I have found if I am enduring a circumstance in my life or waiting for some desire, it takes forever!

Yet, if I am relishing moments in time, they are fleeting. It is like the weather in north Florida; the hot days are endless while the cool days fly by.

Timing, therefore, is subjective. But there is one thing I have learned; God is in control of it and uses it for His glory and our good. I have seen evidence first hand of this glorious truth.

Why it wouldn't be good if we did

As much as I wish I could control it, I am forced to admit I would abuse it; lengthening the easy seasons and shortening the difficult ones. This, in turn, would only bring harm to others and myself because maturity would be difficult to come by. In my experience, waiting or enduring have precipitated great gain in my character as well as my faith. I see this in the life of David as well.

What did David wait for?

In 2 Samuel 5:4 it says,

David was thirty years old when he became king, and he reigned forty years.

Thirty years of age does not sound old to become a king but when you keep in mind that David was anointed king as a teenager, then this seems like a long time.

David waited roughly 15 years from the time he was chosen by God to succeed King Saul until he actually ascended the throne. Not to mention that while he "waited" he was being hunted!

Even as he became King, this was accomplished in stages. He did not claim the throne all at once. The people of Judah first crowned him King but it would take 7 1/2 more years until the remaining tribes of Israel pledged their allegiance.

The time it took for his anointing to become a reality, as well as the process of how it occurred, impresses me. One of the many reasons I love David is how he exemplified patience and submission to God.

He did not initiate the fulfillment of God's promise. You never see him trying to make it happen or force the issue. Even after King Saul was killed, David sat still. He exemplified successfully waiting upon the Lord for the timing God determined to fulfill his purpose.

Why did he do this?

I think the priorities, as well as the convictions, of David's life give insight.

These two reasons explain David's success in waiting upon the Lord's timing without taking matters into his own hands

How David was able to wait well

First, in Psalm 16:2, it reveals the driving priority/passion of David's life. It is believed he wrote this Psalm soon after becoming King of all Israel. It says, "I said to the LORD, 'You are my Lord; apart from you I have no good thing.'"

What a statement to be made by someone with a newly acquired kingdom! Although David was now the King of Israel with a kingdom in his possession, what he valued most was his God! That explains why David was able to wait so well. *He valued what he waited for less than who he waited upon.*

He prioritized God above all else in his life. That positioned him to be better equipped for the waiting game of life.

Secondly, Psalm 138:8 says,

> *The LORD will vindicate me;*
> *your love, LORD, endures forever—*
> *do not abandon the works of your hands.*

David was confident that God was always in control of his life and times, regardless of how long some circumstances remained in limbo.

David was able to wait upon God's timing, not hastening his acquisition of the kingdom, because he rested in God's sovereignty and trustworthiness. He knew that he did not need to make it happen because God was fully capable and faithful. This allowed David to trust as he waited, *knowing the hands of his God were in control of the hands of his time.*

How can we wait well like David?

I long to be more like David; content and confident as I wait for God's purpose to be accomplished. Regretfully, squirming can be my norm...

But I am encouraged! By valuing the Lord more than what I wait for and trusting in His wisdom and ability, I too can cease struggling against time; learning to submit peacefully to the hands beyond my control.

Successfully waiting upon the Lord can become our reality as well.

Day 7

Fighting the Battles Beyond our Abilities

(2 Chronicles 13)

Battles and breaking points- I know them well.

It seems you cannot have one without the other. Whatever tries us also hurls us to our limits. But what if you are pushed past your limits? What then?

Life can oftentimes leave us feeling beyond our ability to endure or overcome. We can feel unable to persevere through what stands before us or against us.

In our own sight and calculations, there is just no way out. No way through.

Battles come whether we want them or not. No matter how hard we try to avoid them, they come. They are no respecter of age, person, or innocence. In the end, life is not always fair.

<u>Life is filled with battles.</u>

It seems from my earliest memories I have faced various battles.

Battles from physical, emotional, and sexual trauma have left me feeling scarred for life. I have some scars that can be seen visibly that testify to the trauma, but most are unseen, invisible to all but me. But they are there, leaving me feeling vulnerable, in need of assurance or predictable safety.

But what in this life affords the luxury of security?

Battles are a constant reminder of just how vulnerable we are. When we are overwhelmed with what we face, we are at our weakest. Battles and breaking points are like two sides of the same coin.

Desperate Circumstances

When I read about the battle of Abijah, King of Judah and grandson of King Solomon, I readily sense his desperate circumstances. He faced a battle against all odds in 2 Chronicles 13:1-20.

The kingdom had already been split. Most of the kingdom went to Israel, but God left a small remnant to remain in the lineage of King David.

King Abijah faced a battle in which he was vastly outnumbered. He had 400,000 soldiers but King Jeroboam of Israel had double that, 800,000 troops lined and ready for battle.

How's that for ratios? What's the battle plan for that? Who wouldn't want to just go home in surrender facing those odds?

I remember feeling just as overwhelmed in some recent battles we faced as a family. Having experienced the trauma from earlier years, I was poised for some major "needs" as an adult.

The need for security was premium in my life so when some issues raised for two of our children, it set me on edge. What I faced each day was unpredictable. It felt like I was on a roller coaster. Such peaks and valleys and jerks out of nowhere left me unglued.

I stayed on the verge of tears, completely unable to control or fix our circumstances. To have two trials going on at the same time for years took their toll. I felt helpless against what we faced. Just like King Abijah as he faced odds stacked against him.

What do you do?

What are the weapons of war for a battle you are sure to lose?

Who would predict victory against overwhelming odds?

As I read his story, it reminds me of my own. Sometimes all you CAN do is all you SHOULD do. *Helpless does not have to equal hopeless.*

I recognize the weapons of war that are not hindered by the numbers of soldiers or circumstances out of control.

With these weapons, the odds don't matter. They are regardless.

Eyes to see are key. To view overwhelming circumstances rocks our sense of sight to the core. What we "see" seems impossible.

But as believers in the God Most High, our sight does not bind us. What we see is not necessarily what we get. He counters ALL reality!

The greatest weapon of war that wins battles beyond reason is a faith-filled perspective.

In verse 12, King Abijah implores the opposing King and the men of Israel not to fight against the LORD. He recognizes the sides of the battle; you are either fighting for the Lord or against Him. In essence, this means He is either fighting for you or against you.

Seeing the sides of the battle is fundamental. It is futile to be on the wrong side against God.

When we were going through our battles, I had to continually check my thoughts and actions to make sure they were in keeping with what God required of me. It was so easy to slip into bitterness and anger, despair and discouragement. I had to regularly examine myself to repent, adjusting to His convictions.

Next in verse 13-14, when Judah was being attacked from the front and the rear, it says they cried out to the Lord. *By crying out to God, they recognized who bore the responsibility of the battle.*

The Lord was their leader (verse 12) and because of that they called upon His Name for help. They did not look for other kings or armies for salvation. They did not even rely upon themselves for the sole victory. Because they were God's through His covenant, they were His responsibility to defend and uphold.

As we faced battles in our family where my sense of security was lost, I had to remember who I belonged to and whose responsibility I was. If I was God's, then what threatened me was His problem as much as it was mine.

When I felt most vulnerable, I ran to Him for refuge. I would literally cry to Him about all my fears and troubles, dumping them in His lap because I knew He had promised to sustain me so I was reminding Him of that.

The same verse 14 where they cry to the Lord also shows *they recognized the need in the battle*. It was their responsibility to recognize the moments where they needed more than what they could do for themselves. Some people face their breaking point and in anger raise their fist to God. Judah and their King realized the need to call upon God. They humbled themselves and reaped the reward for doing so.

Our Battle

Our family learned humility the usual way, when we were weak and needy. Battles make us feel so exposed. As we suffered unmoving circumstances, we were stripped bare of all our own possible resources and answers.

Breaking points have a way of humiliation about them. It is humbling to realize your own inability. But in those moments of weakness comes power as we cry out to God.

We cried out through prayer, through fasting, seeking counsel and support from fellow believers. We knew we did not have what it took to make it through. But through our need, God responded.

Later in verse 15, God routed King Jeroboam and all Israel before King Abijah and Judah. God delivered them into their hands despite such overwhelming odds. Why? Verse 18 says it was because they relied upon the LORD. Simple as that, they faced a mountain of odds stacked against them and they overcame. *They rested in their reliance.*

In our lives, we have seen unfathomable advances against the battles we faced as a family. Both of the circumstances we were so helpless in have been changed dramatically, all without our knowledge or abilities to receive any of the credit.

The odds were against us and we faced our breaking points multiple times. But we faced them like the army of Judah; *recognizing the sides, the responsibility and the need in the battles.*

Then, we were able to be like them, *to rest in our reliance.* This reliance brings peace because you have flung yourself on the mercy of the Almighty Father, who loved enough to sacrifice His only Son. Won't He also now uphold and sustain?

The weapons of war for Judah work just as well today.

We know that as a family and I know that first-hand, as I see God changing a fear-filled woman into a mighty fortress of faith and peace. It took years, but we are seeing the delivering hand of our Father, against all odds.

Day 8

Stepping Through a Storm
(2 Chronicles 20)

How do you feel about the immediate future? Do you feel equipped for what is required of you?

Sometimes life can abruptly change, turning turbulent, threatening our peace and tranquility. Life can be going along just fine and then out of nowhere, a storm pops up.

A job loss, a medical test, a spouse leaving, a child rebelling, a friend betraying, all are "storms" that can feel very threatening. Sometimes instead of one big storm, there can be many smaller squalls that hit, leaving us weary from repetitive struggles that never seem to end.

Whether financial challenges, strained relationships, recurring fears, disappointing love life, or even the bumpy transition into becoming an adult, storms big and small are the norm of life.

But what is the best way to respond to such challenges?

Where is the manual to provide a step-by-step process that can help us know how to navigate through? If you are like me, I am not at my best with knee-jerk responses.

A Bible Perspective

King Jehoshaphat, the king of Judah in 2 Chronicles 20:1-30, teaches us practical steps when faced with a storm or season that feels threatening. I think his story gives insight into some of the best responses when feeling ill-equipped for what you are facing in life.

First, resolve to inquire of the Lord.

When a vast army came to make war against Jehoshaphat, he responded immediately to the threat. Verse 3-4 reads,

Alarmed, Jehoshaphat resolved to inquire of the LORD, and he proclaimed a fast for all Judah. The people of Judah came together to seek help from the LORD; indeed, they came from every town in Judah to seek him.

I love how he led the nation to turn first and foremost to the Lord. They did not seek help from another nation or try to figure out for themselves what best to do.

They immediately ran to God for wisdom and help. They turned to Him for answers, admitting their need for the Lord.

Second, remember who God is and what He has already done.

In verses 6-9, Jehoshaphat stands before the people and prays, reminding them the attributes and promises of their God.

He rehearsed what they already knew of God from what He had said and done before during their history as a nation. Jehoshaphat not only reminded the people, but God Himself, what He had said He would do on their behalf.

Third, acknowledge the circumstances.

Here Jehoshaphat lays out the circumstances in verses 10-11, identifying the threat and difficulty they're facing. The king highlights the injustice being suffered. In essence, he is crying out over what has been done to them.

Fourth, look to God with expectancy.

At this point in verses 12-13, the King admits their utter inability to save themselves or determine what should be done. But he ends with their expectancy of Him to intervene. They were looking to God to defend His chosen people.

Fifth, fight against fear and doubt.

Now it is the Lord's turn to respond. In verses 14-17, God tells them not to be afraid or discouraged. He reminds them the battle is not theirs but the Lord's. He instructs them with what to do as He strengthens them with hope and encouragement, seeking to build their faith in Him. He comforts His people with the assurance that He will take care of them. He does expect them to face their enemy, what threatens them, but He reminds them that He will be with them.

Sixth, worship and praise the LORD.

King Jehoshaphat bowed his face to the ground. Soon all the people fell down in worship before the Lord in verses 18-19.

Then they praised the LORD with a very loud voice, singing of their thankfulness.

Notice this worship and praise was done BEFORE the battle even began. They believed God's promises and praised Him before they were delivered. They thanked Him on pure faith while they were still in need!

I won't tell you how the story ends but I will say it will encourage your faith to read it for yourself. I believe it is helpful in strengthening our resolve to persevere when we read about God helping His people through unforeseen crises.

We learn how to respond to storms that confront us, even when those storms catch us off-guard or last for a while. It is a real, practical process that we can implement for ourselves as we plug in our circumstances to these principles King Jehoshaphat models for us.

<u>Your Turn</u>

Take these suggestions and write in your own details on paper or in your prayer journal. Use Scripture verses that pertain to your specifics regarding your storm.

Do this daily until you are able to stand firm in faith through your storm or until you see the delivering hand of God.

This will help you refrain from getting stuck in negative emotions as you journey through this season.

You can prevail, just like Jehoshaphat, and enjoy the peace and rest of God once again!

Day 9

Ears May Hear But Faith Can Stand
(2 Kings 19)

What happens when you hear words that rock your world?

Words that melt your courage, sending panic rolling over you like a terrible storm?

King Hezekiah knows such a moment, and so do many of us.

One of my favorite reasons for reading the Bible happens when I read something that has a profound affect upon me, transforming my perspective and habits thereafter.

The story of King Hezekiah in 2 Kings 19:1-37 is such an example. He ranks very high as one of my heroes of the Old Testament.

This passage in particular describes moments in time that send chills down my spine. Chills for two different reasons…

What He Heard

The first reason is because of what he heard. King Hezekiah was the king of Judah. In the fourth year of his reign, the King of Assyria attacked the King of Israel.

For three years they laid siege to it. When Samaria was finally captured, the Assyrians deported the Israelites, settling them elsewhere.

The Assyrians took over their lands and possessions for themselves. This happened because they had not obeyed the LORD, but violated His covenant (2 Kings 18:9-12).

King Hezekiah heard of all of this, the fall of the other half of God's divided kingdom. So eight years later when the King of Assyria came calling on Judah, Hezekiah knew exactly what was at stake, how critical the threat was.

Both Israel and Judah had been rebuked for years for their rebellion against God, with the first consequences evident as Israel fell in battle and became spoils of war. When they heard that Israel had fallen, their next thought had to be about themselves. If God had allowed that to happen, what would this mean for Judah?

Faithful Living Didn't Preclude the Trouble

King Hezekiah had been faithful before God as he ruled Judah. He was not considered in the same regard as his father, the previous king. He had learned the lessons from his father's rebellion.

It was King Ahaz that shut the doors of the Lord's temple and set up alters of idolatry on the street corners of Jerusalem.

So even though he was not personally to blame for the nation sinning against God, he had to wonder if his efforts to call the people back to their faith was too little too late. Had the nation gone too far to receive the grace and mercy of God?

At first, the Assyrian army attacked and captured the fortified cities of Judah. King Hezekiah sent a message to the opposing king saying that Judah had done wrong and offered a payment to entice them to withdraw. In a panic, he tried to appease the conquering king with humility and gold that he stripped from the doors and doorposts of the temple. (Not his best moment.)

Even after admitting "fault" to the Assyrian King and giving him gold, the king still sent a large army to Jerusalem with a message.

"Just as I have annihilated other countries, now, I am here for you."

Chilling words………

To know what they did about this powerful, brutal nation and to know they were now in their sights, left little to the imagination. As they heard the threat, based in an all too real reality, they were washed in waves of fear and dread.

Who wouldn't be?

<u>Making it Personal</u>

I remember the day that I heard some devastating news. It left me breathless, like I had received a physical blow. It came without anticipation, when I was least expecting it.

The unanticipated has always been difficult for me to handle. I am at my worst when I cannot foresee a challenge. I need time to process, which leaves me at a disadvantage.

Reeling from the unforeseen news, I seek to grab hold of any hope or solution in sight.

And the reality is, sometimes there just isn't one.

That is where I found myself that day as I walked into work.

I remember going into my office in the back and almost being in a panic.

The fear I felt from what I heard was compounded because I knew there was absolutely nothing I could do about the problem facing us. I remember holding onto the counter in the back to steady myself.

Heart racing, mind reeling, I felt trapped, threatened, just like Hezekiah.

Sometimes problems aren't too scary because "ignorance is bliss". But knowing what you are dealing with can make it even more overwhelming.

So when King Hezekiah's officials told him what the field commander had said, he tore his clothes and put on sackcloth as he headed straight for the temple of the LORD.

Why did he thought of the temple?

Because he knew that is where his hope could be found-in the Lord his God. I love how it was King Hezekiah's knee-jerk reaction to run to God for help.

After trying to fix the threat the first time by himself, he learned the better way.

What help could he expect from God- strength to stand against fear and threats, guidance for what to do, and help in doing it.

God provides emotional, spiritual, mental, and physical help to those who seek Him in times of trouble.

In addition to going straight to the temple, he also sent word to Isaiah, the Lord's prophet, asking him to beseech the Lord for help. His immediate response to Hezekiah was from the Lord, direct and to the point.

"Do not be afraid of what you have heard—those words with which the underlings of the king of Assyria have blasphemed me. Listen! I am going to..."

I love how God zeroed in on the challenge and spoke to the solution. He told Hezekiah not to be afraid of what he heard from the enemy, and then He firmly told Hezekiah to "Listen!" to Him instead. He used an exclamation point to communicate His intensity.

It was as if God was shouting and shaking Hezekiah out of his fear and shock back to the reality of His God being greater than the problem.

In essence He was saying," Don't listen to the enemy! Listen to Me!!"

How to Respond

When I see this king run to the Ruler of all kingdoms for help and security, it gives me chills of the relationship I want with the Lord. It speaks of the intimacy and expectation from belonging to such an Almighty God. It is like a child running for the protection of his father's love and care, but the father just happens to be the Creator and Sustainer of the whole universe.

The privilege, the power, the protection are mind-boggling!

So that day at work when I was struck with fear and dread, I ran to the Father just like Hezekiah. Because I had read his story, I knew what to do when my enemy showed himself, seeking to lay siege to my heart and faith.

My ears had heard the message of doom and gloom but because I inwardly ran to the Lord, my faith remained steadfast against the threat. It was a brutal battle as I panicked but tried to remind myself of the Truth I knew from His Word.

I grasped that counter and planted my feet as I remembered verses of power and comfort from the Bible.

It was not I that held fast, but the Word of God held me as I listened to it over and above the words I heard that day.

There is more to learn from Hezekiah, but that is for another day. The chill I feel as I read of a man's steadfast courage against an army who had wiped out so many other nations is why I continually come back to the Bible.

The thrill of faith is found in no other Book that can empower the victory over our enemy. That is why I "Listen!" with intent. I already know it works!

Day 10

Disturbing The Peace

(*Isaiah 26:3,* Psalm 119:165; John 14:27)

It is inevitable...that break in my peace that comes in a moment's notice.

I am going along fine when either a thought or an action, or maybe even a news bulletin flashes to my attention and there goes my peace. I liken it to a rogue wave coming out of nowhere, knocking me off my feet.

What disturbs my peace is irrelevant. The fact that my peace does fluctuate is what matters.

Over the last few years, I have come to discern how I am feeling at a particular moment and connect it with the peace Jesus intends for me to have in my life. If I am feeling fear or anxiety, then I know I have allowed my peace to be disturbed.

Recently when this happened after returning from vacation no less, I implemented what I know helps me in these situations. In fact, I stopped what I was doing as soon as I could to run to my spot on my yellow couch. (This is where brave battles are fought.)

As I set my mind to the practice I know will bring me back to the peace I have come to expect and enjoy, I thanked God for what He provides for all of His children. His peace is unlike anything else and it has become my necessity.

Three things happen in my effort to regain my peace. These steps have become automatic over time, natural in their flow to my response of fear or anxiety

Steps to Regain Peace

First, Recognize–

I have learned that the first step in regaining my peace is to recognize that it has been disturbed. Before, I would mindlessly wallow in the negative emotions, allowing myself to not only be knocked off my feet by the "rogue wave", but to stay down, getting knocked about by other waves of negativity.

Thankfully, what used to take longer to recover has become much faster as I have begun to pay more attention over how my emotions are affecting me. As soon as I start to feel down, I begin to connect the dots of how I am feeling with what has precipitated it. I look to the root cause of what is driving my emotions.

For instance, I recognized the day of returning from vacation, I began to feel badly because of something that was said. That is all it took for my peace to get wobbly on me. Then add in a few other remarks and there my peace is off and flying!

Second, Remind -

As soon as I am aware of my peace being disturbed, I remind myself of the truth about such matters.

> *You will keep in perfect peace*
> *those whose minds are steadfast,*
> *because they trust in you.*
> *Isaiah 26:3*

I know when my peace has been disturbed that I have let something or someone hinder my faith in God. When I am feeling worry, I am in essence being faithless. I doubt God's ability and attention to the matter.

When I obsess over the roles in my life to the neglect of my identity in life, fear and anxiety are experienced. I am a child of God first and foremost. If I allow my role as wife, mother, daughter, friend etc., to gain more of my perspective than my identity as His chosen child, then my peace is lost.

I have learned this lesson the hard way! When He is my focus, I am at peace. Peace is rooted in my trust of Him. He is All-Knowing, All-Powerful and All-Loving. I can trust that!

Third, Read -

Lastly, I have learned to read my Bible to immediately stop the negative cycle. Why?

> *Great peace have those who love your law,*
> *and nothing can make them stumble.*

Psalm 119:165

Peace I leave with you; my peace I give you. I do not give to you as the world gives. Do not let your hearts be troubled and do not be afraid.
John 14:27

The Word is a powerful weapon (2 Corinthians 10:4-5) fighting the war against fear and anxiety. I have found reading His Word brings my peace right back where it should be.

Peace is mine by right as a child of God, redeemed by the blood of the Lamb!

His peace may be mine theoretically but sometimes I have to fight for it to be returned realistically. Fear sends it packing but His Word brings it back.

The rogue waves in life are not under my control, but my responses to them are. I can pop right back up again regaining the peace I am entitled to because of Calvary.

By applying the process I learn from Scripture, I don't have to allow my peace to be disturbed any longer than the time it takes for me to recognize, remind and read!

What about you?

How do you respond to the waves that catch you off guard and disturb your peace? Are you like I was? Wallowing in the tide of negative emotions that can quickly get out of hand?

Try these three steps next time to see if you can recover your peace even sooner. We don't have to settle for thoughts, words, or events to disturb our peace that Jesus intends for us.

By keeping our focus on our identity in Christ and not our roles in life, we can experience His peace that is beyond our circumstances.

Day 11

Casting Our Cares

(Isaiah 37)

The Purpose

I remember learning long ago that whatever my circumstances may require of me is oftentimes what Jesus is trying to teach me.

That principle helps me identify what the point may be of any particular situation. Paying attention to the "goal" is something I need to be reminded of regularly, because it is all too easy for me to lose sight of the forest for the trees.

Say for example I am in a frustrating time, or maybe a fearful time, I ask myself what is most needed. It could be that I need to exercise patience or faith or courage.

I first identity what emotion I am feeling, then I consider what is required of me in order to address that need.

That is usually what helps me face the challenge more productively. Being a goal-oriented person, I bear up under difficulty better when I see a purpose in it.

That being said, I can become easily overwhelmed though at first glance of a trial. But thankfully, I have learned a practical process to help me when I initially encounter a challenge.

The Practice

King Hezekiah in Isaiah 37:14-38 displays in a nutshell how best to respond to that which overwhelms. He faced a challenge that he knew he was unable to handle.

An army came calling that had wiped out many other nations around Judah, and these other nations were much more equipped than they were.

When Assyria sent word to Judah of their intentions to invade their land and bring destruction upon the Israelites, it says that King Hezekiah "received the letter from the messengers and read it.

Then he went up to the temple of the LORD and spread it out before the LORD." (Verse 14)

As I picture King Hezekiah receiving the devastating news of impending war and probable annihilation, I am astounded at how calmly he responded. It was as if he knew just what to do at such a horrifying possibility.

Inspiration gives me goose bumps as I envision him coming into the temple and kneeling in submission and dependence, as he spread that letter before the Lord. It was a literal transaction of bringing that threat to God's attention and handing it over to Him. Hezekiah may have received that threat, but he transferred it where it belonged!

Psalm 55:22 comes to mind as I read this part of King Hezekiah 's story.

> *Cast your cares on the LORD*
> *and he will sustain you;*
> *he will never let*
> *the righteous be shaken.*

That is exactly what Hezekiah did- *he cast his cares*! He did not sit and stew or try to determine how to respond to the threat. He passed it on to the One who cared for him and wanted to bear his burdens.

His knee-jerk reaction was to turn to God immediately and roll that burden off of himself, giving it to the One who was meant to carry his burden.

Psalm 68:19 teaches us this relief of God bearing the burdens of His people.

> *Praise be to the Lord, to God our Savior,*
> *who daily bears our burdens.*

This truth applies to all types of needs, not just threatening ones. I recently used this principle as I was struggling with the temptation of feeling insecure. As I recognized the emotions I was feeling, I immediately turned to God for the equipping I needed to overcome. In essence, I cast my cares upon the Lord and looked to Him for help.

I knew that Scripture was my greatest weapon when fighting temptation, so I went to the Word to look for verses that were applicable. I found Psalm 73:23-26 and I prayed it whenever I felt the negative emotions. It helped me to gain strength and ability to resist giving way to the temptation as I reminded myself of a better perspective.

Casting our cares upon the Lord equips us to prevail, overcoming what threatens us as we tap into His power and strength.

If it worked for Hezekiah then it can work for the rest of us. To His praise and glory, He wants our burdens and I am all too willing to cast Him mine.

What about you? Are you experiencing temptations or trials? Are you struggling to handle them by yourself?

Consider first what is being required of you through the temptation or trial, as God may be using the opportunity for spiritual growth. Then go before the Lord just as King Hezekiah and cast your care upon Him through prayer.

He WILL sustain you, as only He can.

Day 12

When It's Your Turn In The Fire

(Daniel 3)

No one chooses it.

But sometimes you can't escape it.

When you are backed in a corner and the only way out is... *through.*

That's the fiery trial of Daniel 3:1-30 that Shadrach, Meshach and Abednego experienced, as exiles in the foreign land of Babylon. Under the conquering King Nebuchadnezzar, these three men from Judah found themselves where they did NOT want to be.

God had rebuked His nation because of their idolatry toward Him and injustice toward one another. He had warned them time and time again, calling for their repentance and obedience repeatedly over many years.

The people continued in their sin as they ignored His warnings. Finally, the day had come for His judgment to be poured out upon the nation of Judah.

God sent a foreign king from a distant land to conquer Judah and take its people off into captivity.

Through the prophet Jeremiah, the Lord explicitly explained what was going to happen as a result of their sinful, rebellious ways. Jeremiah 5:19 says,

And when the people ask, 'Why has the LORD our God done all this to us?' you will tell them, 'As you have forsaken me and served foreign gods in your own land, so now you will serve foreigners in a land not your own.'

Not all the people of Judah were unfaithful though, but as often happens, consequences are still far reaching. Therefore, some of the exiles were men and women of faith who still tried to honor God with their obedience, even as they lived as exiles in Babylon.

 Such were the three men who found themselves in conflict with an edict handed down by a foreign king. Submission to this edict was encouraged by the threat of being thrown into a blazing furnace.

Shadrach, Meshach, and Abednego refused to obey the edict, which demanded allegiance and worship to Nebuchadnezzar 's image of gold he had created.

This infuriated the king, so much so that he heated the furnace seven times hotter in preparation for these three men.

After questioning them to see if they would buckle under the pressure of losing their lives in a fiery furnace, the men remained steadfast in their refusal to worship the image of gold. They courageously replied in Daniel 3:16-18,

> *Shadrach, Meshach and Abednego replied to him, "King Nebuchadnezzar, we do not need to defend ourselves before you in this matter.*
>
> *If we are thrown into the blazing furnace, the God we serve is able to deliver us from it, and he will deliver us from Your Majesty's hand. But even if he does not, we want you to know, Your Majesty, that we will not serve your gods or worship the image of gold you have set up."*

Not surprisingly, the king had them bound and thrown into the furnace, which was so hot that it killed the guards who took them up for their execution.

So there they were, backed into a corner and the only way out was THROUGH.

God had not rescued them from this moment, even after their courageous stand. But my friends, He had prepared them!!

What those men needed in order to forge through their fiery trial had already been given them AND was ALSO waiting for them! God had compassionately given His Word to His people in order to draw them to Himself and equip them for what they would need in life, no matter what would be required of them.

His Word gives truth, power and perspective that is life-giving and life-sustaining. In and of themselves, they did not have what it took to be that steadfast. It was God working in them, through them that made the difference. He was giving them the faith and courage necessary to step forward into their fiery trial.

God does not just command that we hold tight to His Word for ego's sake. He knows what it will do for us, how it will change us and grow us. But He does not stop there. He also meets us in the fiery trials we have to go through!

Verse 24-25 says that the King leaped to his feet in amazement, asking if there were only three men tied up and thrown into the fire. He goes on to say,

"Look! I see four men walking around in the fire, unbound and unharmed, and the fourth looks like a son of the gods."

That was the Lord Himself, the pre-incarnate Jesus Christ, who was waiting for them in their fire. He gave them His Word to prepare them in advance and now He was granting His presence in the midst of their trial. His Word had already prepared them to know He would be with them as He had promised in Isaiah 43:1-13, as they walked through their fire.

And He was!!

With His Word in their hearts and His Presence by their side, they could walk through together!

Friends, what has you backed into a corner?

What are you walking through? Whether it is infertility, depression, singleness, or maybe even weariness from an unfulfilled desire of your heart, sometimes getting through just seems impossible.

In this life, we don't always pick our circumstances. Sometimes they pick us and all we are left to do is respond.

I can testify of how God equipped me to walk through my own fire. I began to remember what I knew from the Bible about God and His character. I recalled words from Jesus that were life-sustaining, such as how He said that in Him I would have peace even when in this world, I would have trouble. He exhorts us to take heart because He had overcome the world (John 16:33).

Scripture after Scripture flowed into my mind through the work of the Holy Spirit bringing it back to me. But that came from all those times I had already been in the Word for myself.

I also recalled that He had said He was always with me. So I knew, at that most devastating moment, what I needed to know and posses in order to walk through the fiery trial that lay ahead of me.

Whatever has you backed into a corner, where you know the only way out is through, God is able to meet you there.

Through the ministry of His powerful Word and the presence of His precious Son, He can walk you through your fire too!

Day 13

The Recurring Theme of Facing our Fears

(Jeremiah 40-44)

God is patient, but tenacious. Exasperatingly so at times.

Have you ever noticed how He keeps leading you back to where you DON'T want to go? No way, no how!

He is adept at continually bringing us back to where we have to face the unknown. Or worse yet, the known we don't want to face!!

Why?

What is the advantage in having to confront what we are so desperate to avoid? Why can't we abide where it makes us feel safe and secure?

What is there to gain from "risk"?

I know in my own life that control and guardedness are coping mechanisms.

I feel so much better when I can control what is going on around me or when I can anticipate what may be coming to confront me.

What I am least comfortable with is risk, vulnerability. For me to walk into the unknown, where I cannot foresee what is coming, makes me feel insecure.

Maybe that is the point.

Because when there is insecurity, there is then opportunity!

For what you may ask??

For faith!

Trust!

Dependence!

As I read about the remnant remaining in Judah after it had been devastated by the Babylonians, their tendency to gravitate to their perceived "security" and avoid risk reminds me of myself.

Jeremiah 40-44 describes the context of their story with Jeremiah the prophet staying with the remnant when some of the people assassinated the leader the Babylonians had placed in charge.

What Sort of Opportunity?

After Governor Gedaliah had been murdered, the remaining people left in the land ordered to work on behalf of the Babylonians were terrified.

They feared that Nebuchadnezzar would retaliate against all of them because of a few troublemakers taking matters into their own hands. They had already witnessed first hand the siege and ultimate fall of Jerusalem. After living through that, now they were sure their end had finally come! No way would they be spared a second time!

So they went to Jeremiah to ask what they should do. Should they flee the land for the safety and protection Egypt could offer them?

Or should they stay in the land to wait for the Babylonian's response to the chosen governor being assassinated by one of the Jews?

The prophet answers them clearly in Jeremiah 42:7-12. He tells them that the LORD has told them to stay in the land, not to flee from what they fear will be the reprisal.

He reassures them that the Lord will protect them and help them IF they stay in the land.

The promised blessing of safety and blessing is conditional.

They are to stay where they fear but God will intervene on their behalf if they obey.

How many times have they been in this spot?!!

God continually brings them back to the place where they "need" but with the expectation that He will meet that need above and beyond their expectation.

Insecurity was providing opportunity for faith!

Their looking to God for their need instead of seeking to meet it for themselves required them to exercise reliance upon the Lord.

Insecurity was meant to lead them to greater faith!

Greater faith would facilitate greater intimacy with the Lord, which naturally flows into worship. To know Him is to love Him, to raise up voices and hearts full of praise and thanksgiving.

For many of us, we fight with all our might to avoid the risks or insecurities of life. We fight for our right to control and be independent, not relying on others, even God.

We want what makes sense to us. So when God comes along and His will seems contrary to what we view preferred, we are at the same old crossroads.

Will we face our fears and trust Him or will we choose the predictable path of what we perceive better?

Whether it was trusting God to lead them out of bondage while they were in Egypt hundreds of years earlier, or trusting Him to provide food and water in the desert, or protection from enemy nations surrounding them, or delivering the promised land into their hands, *God continually allowed them to face their fears so that they would overcome them as they looked to Him in faith.*

As I read of the Israelites and their recurring theme of facing their fears, it is easy to then understand His work in my life.

Although I would prefer the security of avoiding risk and vulnerability, it is unrealistic, even harmful to my faith and relationship with the Lord. It is contrary to what I truly want more than "control".

I am far enough along in life to realize what I want more than anything, even control and predictability- I want the Lord!

The Choice is Real

And as the Israelites found out the hard way yet again, when choosing disobedience or independence, trust is forfeited, faith is compromised.

They were safer in the secure arms of a loving Father even in the midst of what they feared, as opposed to fleeing for the control and reasoning their own abilities afforded them.

The security found in the Lord is far and above better than anything else can deliver or prevent.

What fear do you find recurring in your life?

Where do you keep finding yourself? Are you at a crossroads where you keep choosing contrary to what God wants for you?

I know that by letting go and letting God direct me, even if it is into perceived vulnerability, I have benefited more than I could have ever anticipated. I finally clued in to why I kept facing my fears and that was when I was able to overcome them, instead of just avoiding them.

God has nothing less than victory for us as we face our fear, if we will follow Him anywhere or remain steadfast where He plants us! It is in obedience to Him and by His side that we are most secure. No matter what!

So the next time you find yourself facing the path ahead that seems obscure, or the path leading where you do not want to go, trust Him anyway. Believe that in Him, you are the most secure.

Day 14

When Being Misunderstood Is Not Important

(Daniel 4)

Some things just grate against my soul; being misunderstood is one of them.

I fight against it so hard at times, hoping that with the right words or explanations, I can make myself clear. I am under the illusion that with enough clarity, there can be understanding.

Honestly, it can be a stumbling block for me. I feel no peace from being perceived "incorrectly", from being wrongly accused or mislabeled.

That is why as I read Daniel 4:1-37, I am amazed at the response Daniel gives at being mislabeled for who he was.

He had been exiled into Babylon, groomed for service to the king in his palace. Being educated and trained for three years for this new role, he entered *the life he never wanted.*

Daniel's Situation

Right from the start, I witness Daniel's peace with his circumstances. He had already been instructed to submit to the exile in Jeremiah 29.

The prophet Jeremiah told the Israelites to yield to what God was allowing because of their sin.

They were informed to willingly go into exile and put forth their best effort to make a life for themselves while they were there. Jeremiah warned them not to fight against it or sabotage it.

Daniel abides graciously with these instructions. He not only submits, he excels at what he is asked to do. Even more, peace personifies him while in Babylon. This in and of itself is admirable.

He looses his homeland and family, but even worse, he looses his identity. Daniel 4:8-9 says,

Finally, Daniel came into my presence and I told him the dream. (He is called Belteshazzar, after the name of my god, and the spirit of the holy gods is in him.) I said, "Belteshazzar, chief of the magicians,"

Daniel never seems to miss a beat as he is mislabeled, wrongly named after a false god, and misunderstood as a "magician". His correct identity and purpose in life are lost in translation so to speak. But what is surprising is how content he is with it!

Nowhere do we read that he fought against being misunderstood, that he tried to relentlessly correct their misconceptions. He accepted it, giving himself fully to meet their needs.

Who does this remind me of?

Jesus personified peace as He accepted being misunderstood on the cross. He was wrongly accused and mislabeled continually, yet He ceased to try and correct the misconceptions while being nailed on the cross. He submitted to being misunderstood, giving His sinless sacrifice for the sins of others.

Some time ago, God convicted me of this as I fought for being correctly "perceived".

He chastened me with the example of Christ. I was reminded that Jesus was not up there on the cross saying, " Alright, let's go over this one more time!! I am not who you say I am nor guilty of what you accuse me! You need to understand that!!"

Instead, He was willing to be misunderstood. 1 Peter 2:23-34 says,

When they hurled their insults at him, he did not retaliate; when he suffered, he made no threats. Instead, he entrusted himself to him who judges justly. "He himself bore our sins" in his body on the cross, so that we might die to sins and live for righteousness; "by his wounds you have been healed."

Jesus knew there came a time when being misunderstood was not important. It was secondary to the will of God.

Daniel understood this as well in his life, and, so must I.

If God is Sovereign, then He could correct misconceptions at any time.

Yet, what I am learning is that sometimes, He has a higher purpose for me than being understood.

It is then I need to be like Daniel and Jesus, accepting of the misconceptions while still giving my utmost for His highest.

Do you find yourself being misunderstood? Are you in turmoil over it?

First, we must all ask God if there is any truth in someone else's accusations or misconceptions. If God offers no correction and the other people are still unable or unwilling to see our perspective, then we must be willing to be misunderstood... and at peace with it like Daniel and Jesus.

To God's glory and grace, we can and we will!

Thank you so much for spending these 14 days with me reading about how God's perspective can impact our perseverance. These lessons are ones I have learned personally, making the difference in my ability to endure when I felt overwhelmed. It is my prayer that through the encouragement of this book, you too can keep moving forward in the strength of the Lord!

I want to leave you with this last exhortation. God is ALWAYS doing something on your behalf. Though you may not readily see evidence of it, it is true nonetheless.

While I was in the midst of dark times with little progress taking place, I look back now and see all that God actually accomplished. Little did I know how much He would do on my behalf. He has turned my mourning into dancing as only He can!

Give Him time, my friend. And press on!!

Want more from Gretchen Fleming?

You can connect with her on her website and on social media.

Website – www.gretchenfleming.com

Facebook – Gretchen Branstetter Fleming

Instagram - @gretchenfollowinghard

Twitter - @followinghard

Pinterest – followinghard